My World of Science

FORCES AND MOTION

Heinemann
LIBRARY

H **www.heinemann.co.uk/library**
Visit our website to find out more information about **Heinemann Library** books.

To order:
☎ Phone 44 (0) 1865 888066
📄 Send a fax to 44 (0) 1865 314091
💻 Visit the Heinemann Bookshop at www.heinemann.co.uk/library to browse our catalogue and order online.

First published in Great Britain by Heinemann Library, Halley Court, Jordan Hill, Oxford, OX2 8EJ, a division of Reed Educational & Professional Publishing Ltd. Heinemann is a registered trademark of Reed Educational & Professional Publishing Ltd.

OXFORD   MELBOURNE   AUCKLAND   JOHANNESBURG   BLANTYRE
GABORONE   IBADAN   PORTSMOUTH NH (USA)   CHICAGO

Designed by bigtop, Bicester, UK
Originated by Ambassador Litho Ltd.
Printed and bound in Hong Kong/China

06 05 04 03 02   06 05 04 03 02
10 9 8 7 6 5 4 3 2   10 9 8 7 6 5 4 3 2 1

ISBN 0 431 13700 5 (hardback)   ISBN 0 431 13706 4 (paperback)

British Library Cataloguing in Publication Data
Royston, Angela
Forces and motion. – (My world of science)
1. Motion – Juvenile literature 2. Force and energy – Juvenile literature
I. Title
531.1'13

Acknowledgements
The Publishers would like to thank the following for permission to reproduce photographs:
Bubbles: Frans Rombout p26; Corbis: pp8, 11, 16, 19, 28, 29; Powerstock Zefa: p10; Rex: p20; Robert Harding: p5; Science Photo Library: Dr Marley Read p6, Maximillian Stock p7; Stone: pp8, 12, 13; Trevor Clifford: pp14, 15, 17, 18, 21, 22, 23, 24, 25; Trip: P Aikman p27, H Rogers p4.

Cover photograph reproduced with permission of R Smith.

Every effort has been made to contact copyright holders of any material reproduced in this book. Any omissions will be rectified in subsequent printings if notice is given to the Publisher.

Contents

Any words appearing in the text in bold, **like this**,
are explained in the Glossary.

What is a force?

A force makes things move. These people are moving a piano. One man is pushing it. The other man is pulling it.

Pulls and pushes are forces. This girl is pushing down on the pedals to make the bicycle wheels move forward.

Mechanical forces

This bulldozer is pushing earth and trees out of the way. Machines have **engines** that make the force to move heavy loads.

This crane is lifting a heavy load. The engine winds in the cable. The cable pulls up the load. How will the crane move the load?

jib

cable

Natural forces

Wind and moving water are powerful **natural** forces. Wind is air that is moving. It can bend trees and push leaves through the air.

Moving water pushes
things along. This boat
is floating down the
river. The moving water
pushes the boat along.

Moving your body

We use our **muscles** and **bones** to make our bodies move. This climber is pushing and pulling herself up the steep rock.

You can move in many different ways. This woman is swimming. She is using her arms, legs and feet to move herself through the water.

Stopping

Forces can also be used to stop something moving. This dog wants to move forward. Its owner is pulling it backwards.

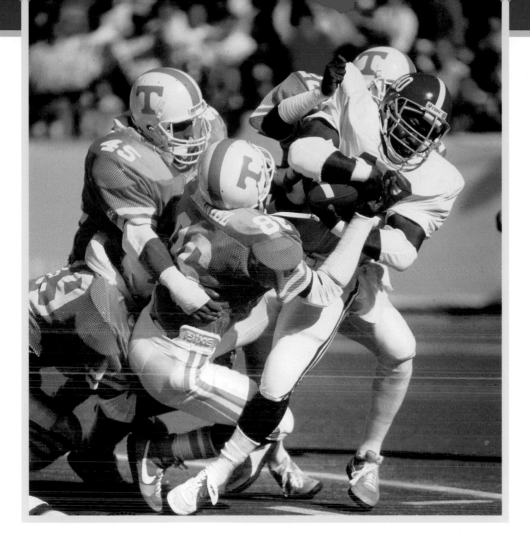

When you push or pull against something that is moving, it can slow it down or stop it. The players in yellow are pulling the one in white, to stop him.

Changing shape

Forces can be used to make some things change shape. Soft putty is easily pushed and pulled into many different shapes.

This boy is squashing the empty carton to push out the air. This makes the carton flatter and smaller. Now it will take up less space in the dustbin.

Changing direction

Forces can make something change direction. This tennis player pushes his racquet against the ball to send it back across the net.

Forces can also make something turn in a circle. You have to twist the top of a jar one way to get it off, and the other way to put it on.

Getting faster

The harder you push something, the faster it moves. This girl is pushing a toy train across the floor. If she gives it a big push, it will move faster.

These runners are working hard to run as fast as they can. Their feet push down and backwards on the ground to move them up and forwards.

Slopes

A slope can change how fast something moves. This girl is skateboarding down a slope. The **steeper** the slope, the faster she will move.

This girl is pushing her wheelbarrow up a slope. She will have to push harder than she did on flat ground.

Friction

Friction is a force that slows things down. The boy pushes the digger and then lets go. The digger moves quickly at first, then slows down and stops.

The digger slows down because the wheels rub and stick against the ground. This is called friction. How many wheels are rubbing against the ground?

Testing friction

This boy is using balls and a **ramp** to test which kind of floor has the most **friction** – carpet, **lino** or wood.

He measures how far the ball rolls before it stops. He finds that it rolls furthest on lino. Does the ball roll further on carpet or on wood?

Using friction

You can use **friction** to slow yourself down on a slide. Push your arms and feet against the sides of the slide – the friction will slow you down.

Bicycle brakes use friction to stop the wheels spinning. When you pull the brake handle, two rubber blocks rub against the wheel.

More and less friction

The **soles** of your shoes are **rough**. They make more **friction** between your feet and the ground. Friction stops you slipping when you move your feet.

The less friction there is, the more you slide. Snow is very smooth and has very little friction. Skiers slide fast across the slippery snow.

Glossary

bone hard part inside your body that gives your body its shape

engine something that uses electricity or fuel, such as petrol or diesel, to make a machine move

friction rubbing between one object and another that slows movement down

lino smooth material used to cover a floor

muscle part of your body that helps you move

natural something made by nature, not people or machines

ramp slope

rough bumpy or uneven

sole the bottom of a shoe

steep when a slope rises or falls very sharply

Answers

Page 7 – Mechanical forces

The crane's engine will move the wheels to move the crane and its load. It can also move the jib to one side or the other.

Page 23 – Friction

Four wheels are rubbing against the ground.

Page 25 – Testing friction

The ball rolls further on wood than on carpet, so wood has less friction.

Index